To Be Covered or Not to Be Covered

Should the world see your glory or God's Glory?

A Verse-by-Verse Discussion about
1 Corinthians 11:1–16

An Elect Chance

WESTBOW·
PRESS
A DIVISION OF THOMAS NELSON
& ZONDERVAN

WestBow Press books may be ordered through booksellers or by contacting:

WestBow Press
A Division of Thomas Nelson & Zondervan
1663 Liberty Drive
Bloomington, IN 47403
www.westbowpress.com
1 (866) 928-1240

ISBN: 978-1-4908-1549-7 (sc)
ISBN: 978-1-4908-1550-3 (e)

Library of Congress Control Number: 2013921010

Printed in the United States of America.

WestBow Press rev. date: 3/31/2014

To my dad, the late Pastor Rudolph Beaconsfield Chance, and my mom, Prophetess Lottie Chance, who through God's grace is still with us and whose love, guidance, and teachings have made me the woman, wife, sister, mother, and child of God that I am today.

Contents

Introduction

No one seems to know why, but one of the most contro-
versial topics in the Scriptures and one that I personally
believe is very important is that of "the covering" found
in 1 Corinthians 11:1–16. I have not heard this topic so much as
mentioned by the Christian leaders that are on television. Neither
does it seem to be taught in the majority of churches today.

What I have seen in some churches is the practice of wearing a hat,
prayer cloth, a chapel cap, or something on the head that symbolizes
a covering. However, actual teachings on "the covering" I have
heard only from one place—my home church, Fishers of Men
Campaigners Inc., under the leadership of my dad, the late Pastor
Rudolph Beaconsfield Chance, and my mother, Prophetess Lottie
Chance. It is now "Fishers of Men Deliverance Ministries Inc.
International," under the leadership of my older brother, Bishop
Reuben B. Chance, the eldest of their ten children.

Now, don't get me wrong. I am sure that there are churches out
there that are teaching this topic (at least I pray that there are).
However, I have visited quite a number of churches and have asked
several women why they cover their heads, and the general response

is the same: it was a custom of their church. This was as far as their explanation went. Very few actually stated that they were wearing a covering because of being obedient to the Scriptures.

In 2009, a holy convocation was being held at Bethel Born Again Church in Kingston, Jamaica—a church that we fellowship with periodically. Rehoboth Church of God in Christ Apostolic, under the leadership of Bishop Keith G. Allen and the late Mother and First Lady Gloria Allen, two wonderful and anointed servants of the Most High God, extended an invitation for my mom and me to attend that holy convocation with them.

The first thing that I noticed when we arrived at the church was that all the women were covered, and they were actually covered in a way that I have only seen in one other place—Guyana, South America at the Christian Mission Church. They wore hats they made themselves or that were made by one of the missionaries in the church. This hat allowed the hair to be completely covered, or they wore a scarf wrapped around their head in the same manner, covering all of their hair. They believed that women should wear a covering in church that would cover all their hair, whether long or short. This belief is based on 1 Corinthians 11:1–16.

I first attended the Rehoboth Church of God in Christ Jesus Apostolic back in 1973. As long as I can remember, the women in Rehoboth Church were always covered. They did not have a set way that they covered their heads (as the apostle Paul did not dictate a specific way that women should cover their heads), but they were all covered. Some of the women wore different types of hats, while others, such as the younger females and children, wore a prayer cloth or chapel cap. This was the practice back in 1973 and is still practiced today at Rehoboth Church.

In several other churches I visited, the hat seemed to be a fashion statement. I think the bigger the hat, the more anointing you were supposed to have. (Just kidding.) There were other churches where the women did not wear a covering, and when I questioned them about this, they stated that they did not have to cover their heads because their hair was "the covering" and that this practice was scriptural.

Another group taught that covering the head was a custom for the Corinthians and that the apostle Paul was only addressing "them," so it does not apply to us today. Well, the apostle Paul was addressing the Corinthians in 1 Corinthians 11:1–17, and he was also addressing them during the other half of 1 Corinthians 11. The last half of the chapter speaks of Communion, so are we to disregard this important part of worship and say that Communion applies only to the Corinthians? How do we decide today as to what applies and what does not apply?

Basically, it comes down to this: what does the Bible teach us about the covering? There are many interpretations concerning this topic, but what about the following two verses found in 2 Timothy 3:16–17, which reads, All scripture is given by the inspiration of God, and is profitable for doctrine, for reproof, for correction, for instruction in righteousness: That the man of God may be perfect, thoroughly furnished unto all good works. So, if all Scripture is given by the inspiration of God, then God allowed Paul to write this letter and included it in the Scriptures not only for the Corinthians but for all the churches of God, then and now. Further, the Scriptures were given by the inspiration of God but were and are also profitable for doctrine. Therefore, this topic must be taught in the churches, because the doctrine of the church is what you follow and live by when you are a member of the church. Do we agree?

3

If your church has a doctrine that is not supported by the Bible, and you are following that doctrine, then you should be able to get an explanation from your leader as to why your church has such a doctrine. If your church is one of the churches of God, shouldn't it follow the guidelines of the Bible? After all, the Bible is our instruction manual. Paul said the Word of God is profitable for "reproof and correction." Many of his letters, whether to the Romans, Ephesians, Philippians, Corinthians, or to the saints and faithful brethren at Co-los-se, were used for reproof, admonishment, and improvement in certain areas. His instruction was in righteousness, which equipped them with what was needed to live right.

Perhaps we should be allowed to pick and choose what we follow and what we can simply ignore. God is coming for a church without spot or wrinkle. Paul wrote to the saints in Galatia, warning them concerning those that would trouble the members of the church and pervert the gospel. Galatians 1:6–9 reads,

> I marvel that ye are so soon removed from him that called you into the grace of Christ unto another gospel: Which is not another; but there be some that trouble you, and would pervert the gospel of Christ. But though we, or an angel from heaven, preach any other gospel unto you than that which we have preached unto you, let him be accursed. As we said before, so say I now again, If any *man* preach any other gospel unto you than that ye have received, let him be accursed.

Paul went as far as to say to them that, if an angel from heaven preached any other gospel to them than what he and the other apostles preached, "let him be accursed."

Therefore, if it is the doctrine of your church for your head to be covered, you should cover your head. However, you should know why (through the Scriptures) you are doing it. And likewise, if the doctrine of your church is for you not to be covered, you should also know why (according to the Scriptures) your head should not be covered. However, the Scriptures do not contradict themselves; they will not tell one group to cover its head and tell the other that hair is a covering. The Scriptures are the inspiration of God and are profitable for doctrine.

Paul concluded by saying, "If anyone seems to be contentious we have no such custom neither do the churches of GOD." Do you see the oneness he was implying? I am not speaking of the Godhead at this moment; I am speaking of the believers in the churches of God. Paul was addressing the Corinthians, introducing the reason for the covering, not the covering itself. I say this because it was already a custom for women in general to be covered. However, it was a custom for the heathen priestess to pray to their god uncovered. Paul wanted the Corinthians to know that the holy women of God are different from the heathen priestess, even in the manner in which we pray and offer our sacrifice to God. Remember, every Scripture is also instruction in righteousness.

Maybe you have read in the Scriptures that your head should be covered, and you believe you should do it, but you are in an assembly that does not teach the need for covering the head. Then you should speak with the leader of your assembly and discuss your views on this issue.

Finally, I encourage all of you as Paul said in 2 Timothy 2:15: "Study to show thyself approved unto GOD, a workman that needeth not to be ashamed, rightly dividing the word of truth." My prayer for all my sisters and brothers in the body of Christ is that you seek the Lord Jesus concerning this topic and that you be obedient to what God is saying to you.

I have included 1 Corinthians 11:1–16 in five of the more familiar versions to assist you with your studies of this topic and to show you that the translators do agree concerning this subject.

Contentions

1 Corinthians 11:16

One contention women make about the covering is that the focus on honoring the Lord Jesus is removed and placed on the woman's hair, her subjection to her husband, and her head being covered. Whenever 1 Corinthians 11:1–16 is mentioned, many think of the covering for the woman and not of the spiritual chain of command that the apostle Paul brought to our attention. Outside of my home church, I don't think I have ever heard this passage of Scripture mentioned in regard to honoring the Lord Jesus. In fact, it is mentioned very briefly. What is said is usually something like "The woman should cover her head to show that she is under subjection to her husband, because this is pleasing to the Lord." They leave you no room for questions, because perhaps they do not have the answers.

Why did I start with verse 16? I thought that I should start here because the apostle Paul's concluding thought is that we should not argue about this: the custom that all the churches of God have is that the women cover their heads during worship, showing honor to their husbands and to God. Paul began by reminding the

Corinthians of the chain of spiritual command: the head of the woman, the head of the man, and the head of Christ. However, it is exactly what many churches have done concerning this topic; they have argued about it, and those who have not argued have simply ignored it completely.

I believe that where some of us have gone wrong is we have forgotten that when we are born again, we have a new life to live. We are now living in the kingdom of God, and there are kingdom principles that we must live by. If we want to please God, we must follow these principles—not just the ones that suit us, but all—especially if we want to please our Lord and Savior Jesus Christ by honoring our husbands.

If we understand this passage of Scripture the way the apostle Paul meant for us to understand it, we will have one point of view, because it's about one point, and that point is honoring the Lord Jesus. This is the reason Paul stated in verse 16, "If anyone seems to be contentious we have no such custom neither do the churches of GOD." In other words, the churches of God everywhere understood the importance and practice of giving honor to the Lord Jesus in their worship.

In order for us to get back to the understanding that it is all about honoring the Lord Jesus, we have to put everything back into perspective. We have to go back to 1 Corinthians 11:3–4: "But I want you to know and realize that Christ is the Head of every man, the head of the woman is her husband, and the head of Christ is God. Any man who prays or prophesies (teaches, refutes, reproves, admonishes, and comforts) with his head covered dishonors his Head (Christ)" (AMP). The rest of the chapter hangs on these two verses. The manner in which we pray or communicate to God either honors or dishonors God.

The apostle Paul gives us a clear picture of how to honor God in our prayer and how we would dishonor Him. Paul started with the man. Why? Because the man is the "image and glory of God, the man stands in the place of God, he is the true representation of the image and glory of God." Therefore, our focus should be on the glory of God, not the man's or woman's glory. In case you did not know this, the woman is the glory of the man, and the woman's hair is a glory to her.

Have you ever stopped to think that Paul started 1 Corinthians 11 by praising the saints in Corinth for "keeping the ordinance"— the teachings or traditions that he delivered to them? Then he went on to instruct them in the order of authority before teaching them concerning the covering. Then Paul ended his teaching on honoring God by saying in 1 Corinthians 11:16, "Now if anyone is disposed to be argumentative and contentious about this, we hold to and recognized no other custom [in worship] than, nor do the churches of God generally" (AMP). And here it is in other versions:

- If anyone wants to argue about that, we don't have any other practice. And God's churches don't either. (NIRV).
- But if any man seemeth to be contentious, we have no such custom, neither the churches of God. (ASV).
- But if anyone wants to argue about this, I simply say that we have no other custom than this, and neither do God's other churches. (NLT).
- But if any man seem to be contentious, we have no such custom, neither the churches of God. (KJV).

Have you noticed that all the translations agree that the churches of God have no other custom in worship? Paul was saying that the saints or churches of God—men and women alike—do not have a custom in dishonoring God during prayer or while they are prophesying.

One thing I do know is that the Devil has always tried to take the place of God. It is recorded in Isaiah 14:12–15,

> How art thou fallen from heaven, O Lucifer, son of the morning! How art thou cut down to the ground, which didst weaken the nations! For thou hast said in thine heart, I will ascend into heaven, I will exalt my throne above the stars of God: I will sit also upon the mount of the congregation, in the sides of the north: I will ascend above the heights of the clouds: I will be like the most High.

Not only did the Devil want to be in the place of God, but he also wanted to be worshiped as God. This is found in Matthew 4:8–10:

> Again, the devil taketh him up into an exceeding high mountain, and sheweth him all the kingdoms of the world, and the glory of them; And saith unto him, All these things will I give thee, if thou wilt fall down and worship me. Then saith Jesus unto him, Get thee hence, Satan: for it is written, Thou shalt worship the Lord thy God, and him only shalt thou serve.

Satan failed at his attempt to be like God. And because of his failure to be like God, he attempted to steal the praise and worship that is rightfully God's.

The Devil has assigned spirits of deception and contention to this topic. These spirits were assigned to deceive the saints in the churches of God. Therefore, wherever praise and worship is to be given to God, if the Devil can steal it, he certainly will. This topic has always been very important to the saints in the body of Christ—not only when the apostle Paul addressed the saints at Corinth, but also today. As men and women of God, we need to know how we must worship and give praise to our God.

I often heard Prophetess Chance ask the women in our church during our women's fellowship, "Now that you have committed your life to the Lord Jesus, who do you want to be in the body of Christ?" Of course, in the beginning, this sounded like an odd question, but she went on to tell us that Jesus is coming for "His bride." According to the book of Revelation, "His wife hath made herself ready." Revelation 19:7 says, "Let us be glad and rejoice, and give honor to him: for the marriage of the Lamb is come and his wife hath made herself ready."

Then she asked us again, "Who do you want to be in the body of Christ?" Do you want to be the bride or just a guest at the wedding?" Now this question begins to make sense. She told us that if we are to be the bride of Christ, then our lives will be more sacrificial than others, and more will be expected of us than those who are just guests at the wedding.

In Roman 12:1–2, Paul wrote, I beseech you therefore, brethren, by the mercies of God, that ye present your bodies a living sacrifice, holy, acceptable unto God, which is your reasonable service. And be not conformed to this world: but be ye transformed by the renewing of your mind, that ye may prove what is that good, and acceptable, and perfect, will of God.

Prophetess Chance, on the other hand, used a natural wedding as an example: She said the bride looks completely different than anyone else at the wedding. At most weddings, you will find maids of honor and bridesmaids. More than likely, they are beautifully dressed, perhaps in what the bride has instructed them to wear. Nevertheless, none of them are the bride. The bride is still the only one getting married. She is the only one that will be exchanging vows with the bridegroom. She is the only one leaving with the bridegroom at the end of the marriage ceremony. The bride is the only one that will become one with the bridegroom.

Prophetess Chance went on to say that while the bride is adorning herself with her wedding garments—her gown and her veil—making herself ready for marriage, she is thinking only of pleasing the groom. So in seeking to please God, her life is now an example for the rest of the body of Christ. This brings me back to asking this question: Why should there be any contention? A women needs to understand who the man represents—and not just their husband, but every man, as it say in 1 Corinthians 11:3: But I would have you know, that the head of every man is Christ; and the head of the woman is the man; and the head of Christ is God. Do you follow me? The head of every man is Christ. Therefore, if we see the man as a representative of Christ, it should be easy for us to honor and respect the man. In turn, we will be honoring and respecting Christ.

This is the principle on which the rest of the chapter stands: Who is the head of the woman? Who is the head of the man? And who is the head of Christ? However, if we are distracted from this principle, we will miss the reason we are being asked to do this simple task. Yes, it is a simple task. Isn't it amazing that we can do something such as wear a hat, put on a veil, wrap our heads as a fashion statement, or cover up a bad hair day? But the minute we are told that we must do it to honor the man or Christ, we have a problem. If you find yourself having this issue, ask yourself, *Why is it that I have this issue?* Some jobs require you to wear something on your head, and if you want that job, you have to comply without coming up with a reason why you can't. We do not seem to have a problem honoring our bosses at work; we will do whatever is "company policy" Well, the church of God has a "company policy." We honor God by being obedient to His will, and, it is God's will that we honor the man. How can we be contentious about any of this?

After Prophetess Chance used this example over a dozen times, the women in our church not only wanted to be the bride of Christ, but we understood that we must be different from the world and different from those in church who are not living according to kingdom principles. We must stand apart from those who are satisfied with being a guest at the marriage of the Lamb. We may be at risk of being criticized, laughed at, and misunderstood, but we cover our heads because we want to be the bride of Christ. This is but a small part of our reasonable service. This is a small sacrifice on our part, and it shows our obedience and willingness to do whatever we need to do to please the Lord Jesus. We will keep the ordinances that were and are delivered to us.

Hair versus Covering?

1 Corinthians 11:15

The apostle Paul stated in 1 Corinthians 11:15, "But if a woman have long hair, it is a glory to her: for her hair is given her for a covering." I believe that many women who do not want to keep the "ordinances" in the first place use this verse to do what they please. Some of us sit for hours when getting our hair done, just to get that right look. How often do we spend hundreds of dollars to have that right look? And when you spend that much on your hair, how can you cover it up? However, this is where rightly dividing the word of truth comes in. Now, the apostle Paul stated in 1 Peter 3:1–6,

Likewise, ye wives, be in subjection to your own husbands; that, if any obey not the word, they also may without the word be won by the conversation of the wives; While they behold your chaste conversation coupled with fear. Whose adorning let it not be that outward adorning of plaiting the hair, and of wearing of gold, or of putting on of apparel; But let it be the hidden man of the heart, in that which is not corruptible, even the ornament of a meek and quiet spirit which is in the sight of God of great price. For after this manner in the old time the holy women also, who trusted in God, adorned themselves, being in subjection unto their own husbands: Even Sara obeyed Abraham, calling him lord; whose daughters ye are, as long as ye do well, and are not afraid with any amazement.

We see here that the apostle Peter is encouraging the holy women of God not to be so concerned with adorning the outward body. Therefore we should concentrate on the hidden man of the heart and adorn our spirit with meekness and quietness. When God sees this (because He sees and judges our heart), we become precious in His sight. The apostle Peter says, "This in the sight of God is of great price."

Apostle Peter was not creating some new doctrine; he reminded us in verse 5 that in the past the holy women who trusted in God adorned themselves in this manner. He went on to say in verse 6 that we are daughters of Sara (spiritually); therefore we should make her our example rather than what we see on TV or on those dummies (manikins) we see in the stores. The world should not dictate how we look. I think it is safe to say that Peter was taking the attention off the hair and putting it back to where it should be in the first place—your spirit. What I see in the verse is that Peter and Paul were in agreement with the order of God. Now, if your spirit is right, you will not have a problem being obedient to God spiritually and physically, nor will you mind reflecting it outwardly. God said He will make a difference between holy and unholy, and we should make sure the world sees that difference in and on us.

So, what do we do with our hair? The first part of verse 15 of 1 Corinthians 11 states, But if a woman have long hair it is a glory to her. Typically we know that women grow or keep their hair long, while men on the other hand wear their hair short. Long hair is given to the woman for "a covering." If I remember my English teacher correctly, *a* is an indefinite article; therefore if Paul said that her hair was given to her for "the covering," then that would settle it, because *the* is a definite article.

The following show the meanings of the words *cover, covered,* and *covering* in 1 Corinthians 11.

- 1 Corinthians 11:4 "Covered" Greek *Kata kata*
- 1 Corinthians 11:6, 7 "Covered" Greek *Kata Kalupto*
- 1 Corinthians 11:15 "Covering" Greek *Peribolaion*
- 1 Corinthians 11:5, 13 "Uncovered" Greek *Akata Kaluptos*

I would also like to add what W. E. Vine says in his *Expository Dictionary* about cover and the covering. I have included not just what is related to our studies—the words *adorn, adorning, cover,* and *covering,* but also everything that he has to say on those words so that you are able to do an in-depth study of those words for yourself.

COVER, COVERING
A. Verb.

1. KALUPTŌ (καλύπτω), signifies to cover, Matt. 8 : 24 ; 10 : 26 ; Luke 8 : 16 ; 23 : 30 ; Jas. 5 : 20 (R.V.) ; I Pet. 4 : 8 ; to veil, in 2 Cor. 4 : 3 (R.V. ; A.V., "hid"). See HIDE. ¶
Note: Cp. the corresponding noun kalumma, a veil, 2 Cor. 3 : 13, 14, 15, 16. See VEIL. ¶
2. EPIKALUPTŌ (ἐπικαλύπτω), to cover up or over (epi, over), is used in Rom. 4 : 7, lit., 'whose sins are covered over.' ¶ Cp. epikalumma, a cloke, I Pet. 2 : 16. ¶

3. PERIKALUPTO (περικαλύπτω), to cover around (peri, around), e.g., the face, and so, blindfold, is translated "cover" in Mark 14 : 65, "blindfold" in Luke 22 : 64. In Heb. 9 : 4, it signifies to overlay. See BLINDFOLD, OVERLAY. ¶

4. SUNKALUPTO (συγκαλύπτω), lit., to cover together ; the sun-, however, is intensive, and the verb signifies to cover wholly, to cover up, Luke 12 : 2. ¶

5. KATAKALUPTŌ (κατακαλύπτω), to cover up (kata, intensive), in the Middle Voice, to cover oneself, is used in I Cor. 11 : 6, 7 (R.V., "veiled"). ¶

Note : In I Cor. 11 : 4, "having his head covered" is, lit., 'having (something) down the head.'

The Greek meaning for the word *covered* found in I Corinthians 11 : 15 means "garment" or "vesture." This meaning is also found in the book of Hebrews and in the book of Psalms. Hebrews 1 : 10 – 12 reads,

"And, Thou, Lord, in the beginning hast laid the foundation of the earth; and the heavens are the works of thine hands: They shall perish, but thou remainest: and they all shall wax old as doth a *garment*; And as a *vesture* shalt thou fold them up, and they shall be changed: but thou are the same, and thy years shall not fail" (emphasis added).

This Scripture is actually a quote from the book of Psalms.

Let's see what David has to say; perhaps this will shine a little more light on our text.

In Psalms 102:26, David stated, "They shall perish, but thou shall endure: yea, all of them shall wax old like a *garment*; as a *vesture* shall thou change them, and they shall be changed" (emphasis added). Wow, do you see what I see? Long hair was actually given to the woman for a vesture or a garment. This is perhaps why my dad would sometime mention that the women in biblical times, because they often bathed outside, probably used their hair as a cloak to cover their bodies. He said when women bathed, they would have their maidservants keep watch in order to warn them if any man was in the area. If a man was seen, the women would shake their hair out, and their hair was long enough to cover their bodies, including all their private parts.

My dad also referenced this Scriptures, showing women bathing or washing in public: Exodus 2:5. This is in the story of Moses when his mother hid him as a babe from the commandment of Pharaoh to kill every male child among the Hebrews. The daughter of Pharaoh came down to wash herself at the river; she and her maidens walked along the riverside. And when she saw the Moses' basket among the reeds, she sent her maid to fetch it.

In 2 Samuel 11, we read another story with a woman bathing. King David was on his rooftop when he saw Bathsheba, Uriah's wife, bathing. Now Uriah (referred to as Uriah the Hittite in 2 Samuel 11) served in King David's army, and he was very honorable and committed to David. "And it came to pass in an evening-tide, that David arose from off his bed, and walked upon the roof of the king 's house: and from the roof he saw a woman washing herself; and the woman was very beautiful to look upon."

And there are a few other Scriptures in the New Testament that tell the story of a woman who used her hair to wipe the feet of Jesus. Her hair was long enough to anoint Jesus' feet.

- "And stood at his feet behind *him* weeping, and began to wash his feet with tears, and did wipe *them* with the hairs of her head, and kissed his feet, and anointed *them* with the ointment" (Luke 7:38).
- "It was that Mary which anointed the Lord with ointment, and wiped his feet with her hair, whose brother Lazarus was sick" (John 11:2).
- "Then Mary took a pound of ointment of spikenard, very costly, and anointed the feet of Jesus, and wiped his feet with her hair: and the house was filled with the odor of the ointment" (John 12:3).
- "And he turned to the woman, and said unto Simon, Seest thou this woman? I entered into thine house, thou gavest me no water for my feet: but she hath washed my feet with tears, and wiped them with the hairs of her head" (verse 44).

Some believe that a woman's head is covered if she grows her hair long and that as long as a man keeps his hair cut short, his head is uncovered. To me, this is making hair the topic of 1 Corinthians 11:1–16. But it is not about hair. It is about the image and glory of God being seen and honoring the Lord Jesus by honoring the man as the image and glory of God. When you understand this you will understand the placement of authority. The apostle Paul mentioned this in 1 Corinthians 11:3: "But I would have you know, that the head of every man is Christ; and the head of the woman is the man; and the head of Christ *is* God." This is what Paul was showing the Corinthians: the placement of authority is God's order. This is important because God set this order, and He placed the man in the position not only as His image but also as His glory.

This brings me to the second part of verse 15, which mentions the word *glory:* "the woman's hair is a glory to her." The last part of the verse includes the word *a*—her hair was given to her for "a covering." The word *glory* was also mentioned in verse 7 when Paul explained why the man was not to cover his head, because he is the image and *glory of God*. But the woman is the *glory of the man*.

The fact that Paul mentions the man not having to cover his head should be proof that hair is not the covering for the woman. First, the man would have to shave the hair off his head in order to honor God when he is praying or prophesying. Second, the definition of the word *glory*, according to *Random House College Dictionary*, is "exalted praise, honor, distinction bestowed on a person or object of pride, absolute happiness, gratification."

Zondervan Pictorial Bible Dictionary states this about *glory* (and this is just a part of the definition):"The exhibition of the excellence of the subject to which is ascribed. Concerning God, it is the display of His divine attributes and perfections. Concerning man, it is the magnification of His commendable qualities, such as wisdom, righteousness, self-control, ability, etc."

The word *glory* is also found 375 times in 44 out of the 66 books of the Bible, and it is recorded twice in the Scriptures that the Lord God said that He will not give "His glory" unto another. Isaiah 42:8 says, "I am the LORD that is my name and my glory will I not give to another, neither my praise to graven images." And Isaiah 48:11 says, "For mine own sake, even for mine own sake, will I do it: for how should my name be polluted? And I will not give my glory unto another."

Now that we have a wider understanding of glory, let's take a closer look at 1 Corinthians 11:4, 6. Three things are mentioned here: *long hair*, *glory*, and *covering*. Let's say for a moment that "hair" is the topic and "the covering." Then we would have to look at verses 4–6 in the following way. Verse 4 would then be "Every man praying or prophesying, having his head covered (or *having hair on his head*), dishonoureth his head." Then verse 5 would read, "But every woman that prayeth or prophesieth with her head uncovered (or *with no hair on her head*), dishonoureth her head." And the last clause of the verse would not make sense, because it reads, "for that is even all one as if she were shaven." If I am standing before you with no hair on my head, just as bald as I can get, will someone say, "Oh, look at Sister Belcher. She looks the same as if she was shaven"? That would not make any sense now, would it?

We see a couple of things happening here. First, the women are praying and prophesying in the assembly. The belief that women were not allowed to pray or prophesy in the temple is unfounded. Luke 2:36–38 states,

> And there was one Anna, a prophetess, the daughter of Phan-u-el, of the tribe of A'-ser: she was of great age, and had lived with an husband seven years from her virginity; And she was a widow of about four score and four years, which departed not from the temple, but serve God with fastings and prayers night and day. And she coming in that instant gave thanks likewise unto the Lord, and spake of him to all them that looked for redemption in Jerusalem.

This woman was a prophetess; she served God night and day, and she did not depart from the temple. Therefore, if she did not depart from the temple but served God night and day with prayer and fasting, she did all this in the temple of God. So those who believe that a woman should not pray or prophesy in church have no scriptural basis for that belief.

What we understand, and what I think we all agree on, is that both men and women will be used by God to minister to His people. However, there is a way God want us to minister to His people. Ephesians 4:11–12 says, "And He gave some, apostle; and some, prophets; and some evangelists; and some pastors and teachers; For the perfecting of the saints, for the work of the ministry, for the edifying of the body of Christ." Also, Philippians 4:3 says, "And I entreat thee also, true yoke fellow, help those women which laboured with me in the gospel, with Clement also, and with other my fellow labourers, whose names are in the book of life."

We see here that Paul acknowledges the women that labored with him in the gospel, so there are several examples of women being active in the assembly of God.

However, I personally believe that because of the "chain of command" or "placement of authority" I mention earlier, women should not be pastors, bishops, apostles, or overseers. I believe that women should be teachers, evangelists, missionaries, and prophetess. This is because the role of a pastor, bishop, and apostle requires one to be the head and to take the leadership role over the congregation—or, I should say, over the people of God. So how can a woman take this position when it is already established that the head of the woman is the man?

Women, this should not disturb you. If it does, take a deep breath and let's go to 2 Corinthians 10:5, which says, "Casting down imaginations and every high thing that exalteth itself against the knowledge of God, and bringing into captivity every thought to the obedience of Christ."

Now let's examine 1 Corinthians 11:3 again and see if you can get a clearer understanding as to why I said my personal belief is that women should not be pastors, bishops, or apostles. The verse states, "But I would have you know that the head of every man is Christ; and the head of the woman is the man; and the head of Christ is God. So the head of both the man and the woman is Christ." Paul continues to say in verse 7 that "the man indeed ought not to cover his head, forasmuch as he is the image and glory of God; but the woman is the glory of the man." Therefore, a woman in the position of a pastor, bishop, apostle, or any position where she sits as head over God's people would not be showing the order that was set in place by God. The man is the head of the woman, and he is the image and glory of God. God wants His image and His glory to be seen by his people. That is His order; therefore the role of the man is to be the head of the people of God.

While I am on the topic of the position a woman may be in, let me just say that any position that causes a woman's attitude or character to change from feminine to masculine or causes her to usurp authority over the man, then I would have to say that this is not a position she should be in.. Further more ladies, saints of the Most High God, I am not saying that you are not capable to operated in any position you choose however, if the position changes you, or you change because of the position then we can safely say that the position is demanding a different type of person to be there or there would be no need for the change. Follow me? Amen.

You see, the word *usurp* is found in 1 Timothy 2:12. In this letter to Timothy, Paul instructs him not to allow the women to usurp authority over the men. Second, according to the Webster New World Dictionary of the American Language, the word usurp means, to take or assume and hold in position by force or without right. In other words to take a position of power or authority, illegally, to take the place of someone in the position of power illegally, or to supplant." Third, the Word of God states in Malachi 3:6, (first part) For I am the LORD, I change not, and seeing we are in His image and likeness, God will not ordain someone to be in a position that would change His image or His likeness. He has created us to be fruitful and multiply and to fill the earth with godly men and women that will live in His order.

Earlier in this same chapter, in 1 Timothy verses 8 –10, Paul wrote, I will therefore that men pray everywhere, lifting up holy hands, without wrath and doubting. In like manner also, that women adorn themselves in modest apparel, with shamefacedness and sobriety; not with broided hair, or gold, or pearls, or costly array; But (which becometh women professing godliness) with good works.

Peter also wrote concerning women adorning themselves and being in subjection in 1 Peter 3:1–5.

> Likewise, ye wives, be in subjection to your own husbands; that, if any obey not the word, they also may without the word be won by the conversation of the wives; While they behold your chaste conversation coupled with fear. Whose adorning let it not be that outward *adorning* of plaiting the hair, and of wearing of gold, or of putting on of apparel; But let it be the hidden man of the heart, in that which is not corruptible, even the ornament of a meek and quiet spirit, which is in the sight of God of great price. For after this manner in the old time the holy women also, who trusted in God, adorned themselves, being in subjection unto their own husbands.

Take note of verse 5: For after this manner in the old time the holy women also, who trusted in God, adorned themselves, being in subjection unto their own husbands.

This verse clearly states that in old time the holy women adorned themselves, being in subjection. If you are a holy woman of God, how you dress is important. Why is it important? Well, first of all, because the man represents Christ and the woman represents the church it is important that we adorn ourselves in a way that pleases Christ. One of the ways we do this is to dress in a manner that shows we are subject to our husbands.

Second, Moses wrote in Deuteronomy 22:5: The woman should not wear that which pertaineth unto a man, neither shall a man put on a woman's garment: for all that do so is an abomination unto the LORD thy God." This verse came to mind when I thought of the woman being on a job or in a position that demands that she dresses in a manner that suits the position she is in, and not dress according to the standard of the holy women of God.

One of the meanings of the word *pertaineth,* according to Webster's Dictionary, is made to be like. However, remember we are to dress in a fashion that professes godliness. A fashion that shows the world we are the church and we are subject to Christ.

What does all this have to do with the covering or with the woman's hair? Well, we all know that how a woman dresses and how she wears her hair, or how she covers her head are all part of her adorning herself. So as holy women of God, we want to please not only our husbands but also the Lord our God.

As I wrote earlier, at the time that Paul addressed the Corinthians, women who worshiped in the pagan temples had their heads shaved. This was to show that they belong to the gods that they worshiped; it marked them as temple whores or prostitutes. This was their way of being in subjection to the will of their god. There should be a difference between holy and unholy. We are holy women of God, and the way we show that we are in subjection to the will of our God is by submitting to His order and chain of command. The lead verse in this entire passage is 1 Corinthians 11:3: "But I want you to know that the head of every man is Christ, the head of the woman is man, and the head of Christ is God."

Many made 1 Corinthians about hair, and I am going to say it again: It is not about hair. It is about headship and the image and Glory of God being seen. Once we fully understand this, we women will not mind allowing the glory of God to be seen by covering our hair, which is a glory to us.

If the position that we are in, is hindering us from showing the world the person that God has created us to be, we are in a position that is causing us to dishonor God. Therefore, we are in the wrong position. We know that dishonoring God is not what we want to do, so then as godly women lets begin to please and honor God by covering our heads.

1 Corinthians 11:1–16

Verse by Verse

erse 1. Paul began by addressing the saints in Corinth and requesting that they be followers of him as he is of Christ. Pattern yourselves after me [follow my example] as I imitate and follow Christ [The Messiah] AMP. Paul was saying to the Corinthians that they should imitate him as he imitates Christ. Okay, I don't see any harm in this. No contention here.

Verse 2. I appreciate and commend you because you always remember me in everything and keep firm the possession of the traditions (the substances of my instructions), just as I have (verbally) passed them on to you. AMP. Paul is now letting the Corinthians know how much he appreciates them for holding on to the traditions that he verbally passed on to them. Seeing that he is going to take almost half of the chapter to speak on the covering, I think it is safe to say that this is one of those "traditions."

Now, did you know that before the law of Moses, there is an example of a woman covering her head? This is found in Genesis 24:64–65: And Rebekah looked up, and when she saw Isaac, she dismounted from the camel. For she [had] said to the servant, who is that man walking across the field to meet us? And the servant [had] said. He is my master. So she took a veil and concealed herself with it. AMP.

Notice that she did not cover or conceal in the presence of Abraham's servant or her brother; she covered herself when she saw the man that was to be her husband. Therefore, the woman covering herself in respect and honor to the man is a tradition. So it is safe to say that Paul was referring to this tradition in 1 Corinthians 11:1–16. I can't think of any reason to be contentious about Paul showing his appreciation to the Corinthians by commending them for keeping him in their remembrance in all things and also keeping the teachings that he had delivered to them.

Verse 3: But I want you to know and realized that Christ is the Head of every man, the head of a woman is her husband and the Head of Christ is God. AMP. Now it is getting juicy. So, let's see: Christ is the Head of every man. This is great; no problem! And the head of a woman is her husband. Should I be contentious about this? Well, let's start at the beginning:

> And God said, let us make man in our image, after our likeness: and let them have dominion over the fish of the sea, and over the fowl of the air, and over the cattle, and over all the earth, and over every creeping thing that creepeth upon the earth. So God created man in his own image, in the image of God created he him; male and female created he them. And God blessed them and God said unto them, be fruitful, and multiply, and replenish the earth, and subdue it: and have dominion over the fish of the sea, and over the fowl of the air, and over every living thing that moveth upon the earth. (Genesis 1:26–28)

And the LORD God formed man of the dust of the ground, and breathed into his nostrils the breath of life; and man became a living soul. And the LORD God said, it is not good that the man should be alone; I will make him an help meet for him. And the LORD God cause a deep sleep to fall upon Adam and he slept: and he took one of his ribs, and closed up the flesh instead thereof; And the rib, which the LORD God had taken from man, made he a woman and brought her unto the man. And Adam said, This is now bone of my bones, and flesh of my flesh: she shall be called Woman, because she was taken out of Man. (Genesis 2:7–18, 21–23)

Wow! Don't you just love the LORD? Okay, I should not have to explain, but I am still hearing someone saying, "What's your point?" So, here it is: In Genesis 1:26–28, when God created the man and the woman, He created them in His own image and likeness, and male and female created He them, He blessed them, He commanded them to be fruitful, to multiply, to replenish, to subdue, and have dominion over everything on the earth. However, we know that God is a Spirit: John 4:24 reads, God is a Spirit: and they that worship Him must worship Him in spirit and in truth. And Job 33:4 states, The spirit of God hath made me, and the breath of the Almighty hath given me life. Therefore, the male and female created in Genesis are spirit being. And we know this because in Genesis 2:7 we read of the man being formed. We know that God formed the male first, because verse 18 says that the man was alone; then in verses 21–23 you get the description of the woman being formed and brought to the man.

It's very important to notice that nothing was said to the woman after she was made. The Lord God spoke to her when He created her in Genesis 1:26–28; He gave her the same commandments that He gave the man, and she was also blessed the same way the man was blessed. However, where was the woman when God was speaking to her? She was still in the man, and the man was still in God. In Genesis 2:15–17 (please read), you see that after God formed man He planted a garden and put man in the garden. He spoke to the man and gave the man another commandment. We know that the woman is there, because He created them male and female and we read where the Lord God took the woman out of the man. Why is all this important? Because when you understand the *placement of authority* that God has put in order and you embrace it, you will agree that there should be no contention over any of these verses.

I could have simply said that if Christ is the Head of the man, the Head of the woman is also Christ, but it is always enjoyable going through the Scriptures, don't you agree?

After Paul established that the head of every man is Christ, and the head of the woman is the man, and the head of Christ is God, in verse 4 he began to speak on how a man can dishonor his head. He addressed the men first by telling them that every man praying or prophesying having his head covered dishonors his head. Keep in mind that the Paul has already established that the head of the man is Christ. Therefore, he is saying that if men pray or prophesy with their heads covered, they dishonor Christ.

Verse 4: Every man praying or prophesying, having his head covered, dishonereth his head. For years I have read this Scripture, and it is always amazing to me that whether I am at a funeral, a wedding, or any type of ceremony where someone is going to pray, I notice that the men everywhere remove their hats—both sinner and saints alike—without being told to do so. However, women who are wearing something on their head—both sinner and saint alike—do not remove it. Is it just a show of respect or by instinct that men remove their covering and women don't, or is it both? This reminds me of the Scripture in the Old Testament when the Lord was speaking to Jeremiah, in Jeremiah 31:33, But this is the covenant which I will make with the house of Israel: After those days, says the Lord, I will put My law within them, and on their hearts will I write it; and I will be their God and they will be My people. AMP. See the section on, "Reasons why a man should not cover his head."

Now, because Paul started with the man, I think that we should start with the man also. If we can get this straight, the rest will fall into place. So, this is where we have to ask ourselves this question: Is Paul speaking to the man concerning his head covered with hair or covered with something else other than hair? So, am I to understand this correctly, "having his head covered" is Paul saying that if a man prays to God with hair on his head, he dishonors Christ? Or is he saying that the man should not have anything covering his head while he is praying or prophesying, such as a hat, a turban, or a hat like a pope or a Jewish rabbi wears? If the topic is hair and hair is the covering that Paul is talking about throughout this text, I would say yes: if a man prays with hair on his head, he dishonors his head which is Christ. However, if hair is not the covering that Paul is talking about, this means that the man should not have anything on his head besides hair when he is praying or prophesying.

Verse 5: "But every woman that prayeth or prophesieth with her head uncovered dishonereth her head: for that is even all one as if she were shaven." As I've stated before, if hair is the covering that Paul is speaking about in this verse, if the woman were to be uncovered, she would have to remove her hair completely. The verse begins with the word *but*, which we know is a conjunction, meaning that this verse is a continuation of verse 4. Therefore, after Paul explains that the man praying with his head covered dishonors his head, (Christ) he said, "But every woman that prayeth or prophesieth with her head uncovered dishourneth her head: for that is even all one as if she were shaven." Here is how verse 5 reads in other versions:

- And any woman who [publicly] prays or prophesies (teaches, refutes, reproves, admonishes, or comforts) when she is bareheaded dishonors her head (her husband); it is the same as [if her head were] shaved (AMP).
- But a woman dishonors her head if she prays or prophesies without a covering on her head, for this is the same as shaving her head. (NLT).
- But every woman praying or prophesying with her head unveiled dishonoreth her head; for it is one and the same thing as if she were shaven. (ASV).

Okay now, this verse shines more light on hair versus covering, don't you think? Let's go over what Paul is saying in this verse, starting with the *Amplified Bile*. Paul clearly states that any woman who publicly prays or prophesies (teaches, refutes, reproves, admonishes, or comforts) when she is bareheaded dishonors her head (her husband). Some may jump the gun (so to speak), thinking that "bareheaded" could mean that if she prays with "no hair on her head" she is bareheaded. But look at the last clause of the verse; Paul says if she prays bareheaded, it is the same as if her head were shaved. Therefore, if bareheaded meant that there is no hair on your head—or, as we say bald—it would not make sense for Paul to say if the woman prays bareheaded (bald) it is the same as if she was shaved. The last time I checked, *bald* and *shaven* had the same meaning.

However, with all the light that was just shone on that verse, if that didn't clear it up for you and you still need more light, take a look at verse 6 starting with the *King James Version.* Here is another conjunction, *for,* so Paul is continuing again from the former verse.

Verse 6: For if the woman be not covered let her also be shorn: but if it be a shame for a woman to shorn or shaven, let her be covered. This is a very important verse because it shows why it is important for women to cover their heads. And it shows what we should do if we are not going to cover our head. Paul explains clearly that if the woman is not covered, she should also shave her head. Do you understand why? Because *her hair is her glory,* it is not her glory to be seen; it is the glory of God to be seen. This is why, if she is not going to cover it, she must remove it—plain and simple. However, Paul reminds them that it is a shame for her hair to be shorn or shaven, because this was the punishment for women found in whoredom and adultery (see Numbers 5:18).

Now, verse 6 reads, "For if the woman be not covered, let her also be shorn: but if it be a shame for a woman to be shorn or shaven, let her be covered." And here it is in other versions:

- For if a woman will not wear [a head] covering, then she should cut off her hair too; but if it is disgraceful for a woman to have her head shorn or shaven, let her cover [her head] (AMP).
- Yes, if she refuses to wear a head covering, she should cut off all her hair! But since it is shameful for a woman to have her hair cut or her head shaved, she should wear a covering. (NLT).
- For if a woman is not veiled, let her also be shorn: but if it is a shame to a woman to be shorn or shaven, let her be veiled (ASV).

Have you notice that in all three versions the translators agree that Paul is talking about something other than *hair* that should be covering the woman's head? In the *Amplified Bible,* Paul clearly states that if the woman will not wear a head covering, she should cut off her hair. So according to this translator, hair is not the covering for the woman's head in this verse. In the *New Living Translation,* if the woman refuses to wear a head covering, she should cut off her hair. Again you see that the translator reveals a difference between the covering and the woman's hair.

Let's see if the *American Standard Version* differs from the others. It states, If the woman is not veiled, let her also be shorn.. Well, this translator also agrees that the woman should have something on her head other than her hair, and if she refuses to cover her hair, she cuts it off; it is the glory of God to be seen, not her glory.

Verse 7: For a man indeed ought not to cover his head, forasmuch as he is the image and glory of God: but the woman is the glory of the man. Now you can understand this verse: it's not about hair. How many times do I have to say it's not about hair, saints? If it is, then all men would have to shave their heads bald to honor God. But because he is the image and glory of God, he is not to cover his head. He represents God, and God wants His people to see Him.

Let's look at this verse again: For a man indeed ought not to cover his head, forasmuch as he is the image and glory of God: but the woman is the glory of the man. We have the woman "being" the glory of the man. That means she is man's glory and her hair is "a glory" to her, or you could say, "her glory." Because it is important that the glory of God is seen and not the woman's glory—or the man's glory, for that matter—Paul could not have said it any clearer when he says that if a woman is not going to cover her glory, then she must cut it off. With her hair cut off, she is no longer the glory of the man; she becomes a dishonor to him because it is a shame for her head to be shaven.

I like the way the *New Living Translation* put it: Yes, if she refuses to wear a head covering, she should cut off all her hair! But since it is shameful for a woman to have her hair cut or her head shaved, she should wear a covering. Women, please, we have several different versions saying the same thing concerning this topic. Are we still going to need revelation from God whether to cover our heads or not?

Verse 8: For the man is not of the woman; but the woman of the man. Genesis 2: 21–23 says, And the Lord God caused a deep sleep to fall upon Adam, and he slept: and he took one of his ribs, and closed up the flesh instead thereof; And the rib, which the LORD God had taken from man, made he a woman, and brought her unto the man. And Adam said, This is now bone of my bones, and flesh of my flesh: she shall be called Woman, because she was taken out of Man. (emphasis added).

Verse 9: Neither was the man created for the woman but the woman for the man. And, as I quoted before,

> And the LORD God said, It is not good that the man should be alone; I will make him an help meet for him. And the LORD God cause a deep sleep to fall upon Adam, and he slept: and he took one of his ribs, and closed up the flesh instead thereof; And the rib, which the LORD God had taken from man, made he a woman, and brought her unto the man. And Adam said, This is now bone of my bones, and flesh of my flesh: she shall be called Woman, because she was taken out of Man. (Genesis 2:18, 21–23)

Verse 10: For this cause ought the woman to have power on her head because of the angels. Angels are ministering spirits ordained of God to minister to us. We as sons of God need to be an example and show that we are in submission to the order of God. Therefore, being in obedience to God's order is functioning in the authority and power of God.

Verse 11: Nevertheless neither is the man without the woman, neither the woman without the man, in the Lord. Remember ladies, Genesis 1:26–28 "male and female created he them"

First, notice the three words "and let them," and you see that the woman was there. Second, "male and female created he them." Third, God bless them. So you see, you can't have man without woman.

Verse 12: For as the woman is of the man, even so is the man also by the woman; but all things of God. Genesis 5:1–2 reads, This is the book [the written record, the history] of the generation of the offspring of Adam. When God created man, He made him in the likeness of God. He created them male and female and blessed them and named them [both] Adam [man] at the time they were created. AMP. So Adam may not have been born of a woman, but every man after him was born of a woman.

Verse 13: Judge in yourselves: is it comely that a woman pray unto God uncovered? Once I understood the placement of authority and why I should cover my head, I did just that. I checked myself to see if I had any contention about it, and there was none. I wanted to be pleasing in God's sight.

Verse 14: Doth not nature itself teach you, that, if a man has long hair, it is a shame unto him? Yes, it does. There was a time that it was shameful for a man to wear his hair long, and just because it is no longer shameful today does not mean it is acceptable in the kingdom of God. Paul wrote in Romans 12:1–2,

I appeal to you therefore, brethren, and beg of you in view of [all] the mercies of God, to make a decisive dedication of your bodies [presenting all your members and faculties] as a living sacrifice, holy [devoted, consecrated] and well pleasing to God, which is your reasonable [rational, intelligent] service and spiritual worship. Do not be conformed to this world [this age], [fashioned after and adapted to its external superficial customs], but be transformed [changed] by the [entire] renewal of your mind [by its new ideals and its new attitude], so that you may prove [for yourselves] what is the good and acceptable and perfect will of God, even the thing which is good and acceptable and perfect [in His sight for you]. AMP.

We are not to be conformed to this world but we are to be transformed by the renewing of our minds.

Why do our minds have to be renewed? Because as Paul also said to the Romans, [That is] because the mind of the flesh [with its carnal thoughts and purposes] is hostile to God, for it does not submit itself to God's Law; indeed it cannot.

So then those who are living the life of the flesh [catering to the appetites and impulses of their carnal nature] cannot please or satisfy God, or be acceptable to Him. AMP. (Romans 8:7–8). Wow! So much is being said in these two verses. Therefore, we have to renew our minds daily by the word of God.

Verse 15: But if a woman have long hair, it is a glory to her: for her hair was given her for a covering. A woman's long hair is a glory to her, not to God. Her hair was given to her for *a* covering, not "*the* covering". If hair is the covering, the man must shave his head, removing all his hair in order not to dishonor his head.

Verse 16: But if any man seem to be contentious, we have no such custom, neither the churches of God. Paul states in Romans 2:5-11,

But after thy hardness and impenitent heart treasurest up unto thyself wrath against the day of wrath and revelation of the righteous judgment of God; Who will render to every man according to his deeds: To them who by patient continuance in well doing seek for glory and honor and immortality, eternal life: But unto them that are contentious, and do not obey the truth, but obey unrighteousness, indignation and wrath. Tribulation and anguish, upon every soul of man that doeth evil, of the Jew first, and also of the Gentile; But glory, honour, and peace, to every man that worketh good, to the Jew first, and also to the Gentile: For there is no respect of persons with God; For not the hearers of the Law are just before God, but the doers of the law shall be justified.

In other words obey the truth and be a doer of the law and not just a hearer.

Reasons the Woman's Head
Should Be Covered

- The woman's hair is her glory, and it is the glory of the Lord Jesus to be seen, and not her (1 Corinthians 11:15).
- Everything that we do must be done to the glory of the Lord Jesus (1 Corinthians 10:31; Colossians 3:17, 23).
- The woman (wives) must show that they reverence (honor) her husband (Ephesians 5:31).
- The woman needed to cooperate fully with her husband and keep the customs, thus showing that she was equally blessed by God (verse 11-12; Genesis 24:65; 38:14, 19; Ruth 3:15; Isaiah 3:23 1 Timothy 2:9; 1 Peter 3:1-7)
- The woman must cover her head as a sign that she is in subjection to her head (Ephesians 5:22–24; Colossians 3:18; 1 Peter 3:1).
- The woman is the glory of the man. Man is the glory of God. Again, it is the glory of God to be seen and not the man's glory or the woman's glory (1 Corinthians 11:7).
- So that she will have power on (with) her head because of the holy angels, in other words, it is a lesson to the angels to continue to submit to God 1 Corinthians 11:10; 4:9; Ephesians 3:10–11; Ecclesiastes 5:6; 1 Timothy 5:21).

- The woman was made to be a helpmeet for the man; therefore she is to help the man in declaring the glory of God (Genesis 2:18, 21–22).
- If the woman understands that she is to cover her head when praying or prophesying and she refuses, she is not worshipping the Lord Jesus in spirit and in truth.
- No flesh shall glory in God's presence (1 Corinthians 1:29).
- God chose man to declare his glory and the woman to declare the glory of the man. God said he will share His glory with no one (Isaiah 42:8).
- When the woman is obedient to this simple action, she not only shows that she is in agreement with the order of God, but she declares her equality, her dominion, and her authority, for neither is the man without the woman or the woman without the man (1 Corinthians 11:2, 8, 9, 12; Genesis 1:26–27).

How do we justify the covering as the symbol of authority on the woman's head?

- First, it is in keeping with the spirit of 1 Corinthians 11.
- Second, if you had to make a choice, would you not rather choose to wear a covering, seeing that Scripture never stated that wearing the covering was dishonoring the man or God?
- Third, another symbolic tradition that Paul handed down to the Corinthians was the Lord's Supper, which is also mention in 1 Corinthians 11, starting with verse 17. Should we say that this is just for the early church and does not apply to us today?
- Fourth, because the actual symbol is not the issues; what it represents is the issue: submission to authority (1 Corinthians 11:5–7).
- Fifth, when Paul addressed the church in Corinth, he spoke to all that call upon the name of Jesus Christ our Lord (1 Corinthians 1:2).
- Finally, in the first book of the bible, even before the law of Moses was written, women covered themselves as a sign of respect for their husbands. (Genesis 24:65)

Reasons the Man's Head
Should Not Be Covered

- 1 Corinthians 11:4: "Every man praying or prophesying, having his head covered, dishonereth his head."
- 1 Corinthians 11:7: "For a man indeed ought not to cover his head, forasmuch as he is the image and glory of GOD: but the woman is the glory of the man."
- 1 Timothy 2:13: "For Adam was first formed then Eve."

Conclusion

I n 1 Corinthians 11:1–16, Paul was clearly given the order in which godly men and women worship in the churches of God. Therefore I refuse to be contentious about this topic, because I am a member of one of the churches of God, and He is the Lord Jesus.

My hair was given to me as *a* covering and not as *the* covering. It is also a glory to me, and I will submit to covering my glory in order for the glory of the Lord Jesus to be seen.

I have judged in myself and I trust the Spirit of the Lord Jesus within me and know beyond a shadow of a doubt that I am to cover my head with a covering (veil) other than my hair, because it is not proper for me to pray to God without a covering.

The Word of God also teaches me that there is to be a difference between holy and unholy. The heathen priestess prayed, prophesied, and delivered the oracles bareheaded or with disheveled hair. I will not conduct myself as the unholy when I was commanded to be holy (Clarke's commentary on the bible).

The woman was created in the image and likeness of God. Just like the man, she was blessed and given the same dominion and authority as the man (Genesis 1:26–28). However, she was made to be a helpmeet for the man (Genesis 2:8, 21–23). The man was first formed, and then the woman (1 Timothy 2:13).

I understand the order of God and the placement of authority. I embrace God's order; therefore I cover my head with a veil to show my submission to the order of God and His placement of authority. In so doing, I remain equal with the man, for neither is the man without the woman or the woman without the man in the Lord.

Appendix

1 Corinthians 11:1–16 in Five Bible Versions

King James Version

¹Be ye followers of me, even as I also am of Christ.

²Now I praise you brethren, that you remember me in all things, and keep the ordinances, as I delivered them to you.

³But I would have you know, that the head of every man is Christ, and the head of the woman is the man, and the head of Christ is God.

⁴Every man praying or prophesying having his head covered, dishonoureth his head.

⁵But every woman that prayeth or prophesieth with her head uncovered, dishonoureth her head, for that is even all one as if she were shaven.

⁶For if the woman be not covered, let her also be shorn, but if it be a shame for a woman to be shorn or shaven, let her be covered.

^{7}For a man indeed ought not to cover his head, forasmuch as he is the image and glory of God. but the woman is the glory of the man.

^{8}For the man is not of the woman, but the woman of the man.

^{9}Neither was the man created for the woman, but the woman for the man.

^{10}For this cause ought the woman to have power on her head because of the angels.

^{11}Nevertheless neither is the man without the woman, neither the woman without the man, in the Lord.

^{12}For as the woman is of the man, even so is the man also by the woman; but all things of God.

^{13}Judge in yourselves: is it comely that a woman pray unto God uncovered?

^{14}Doth not even nature itself teach you, that, if a man have long hair, it is a shame unto him.

^{15} But is a woman have long hair, it is a glory to her: for her hair is given her for a covering.

^{16}But if any man seem to be contentious, we have no such custom, neither the churches of God.

Amplified Bible

¹Pattern yourselves after me [follow my example], as I imitate and follow Christ (the Messiah).

²I appreciate and commend you because you always remember me in everything and keep firm possession of the traditions (the substance of my instructions), just as I have [verbally] passes them on to you.

³But I want you to know and realize that Christ is the Head of every man, the head of a woman is her husband, and the head of Christ is GOD.

⁴Any man who prays or prophesies (teaches, refutes, reproves, admonishes, and comforts) with his head covered dishonors his Head (Christ).

⁵And any woman who [publicly] prays or prophesies (teaches, refutes, reproves, admonishes, and comforts) when she is bareheaded dishonors her head (her husband); it is the same as [if her head were] shaved.

⁶For if a woman will not wear [a head] covering, then she should cut off hair too; but if it is disgraceful for a woman to have her head shorn or shaven, let her cover [her head].

⁷For a man ought not to wear anything on his head [in church], for he is the image and [reflected] glory of GOD, [but his function of government reflects the majesty of the divine Rule]; but woman is [the expression of] man's glory (majesty, preeminence)

⁸For man was not [created] from woman, but woman from man;

⁹Neither was man created on account of or for the benefit of woman, but woman on account of and for the benefit of man.

¹⁰Therefore she should [be subject to his authority and should] have a covering on her head [as a token, a symbol, of her submission to authority], that she may show reverence as do the angels [and not displease them].

¹¹Nevertheless, in [the plan of] the Lord and from His point of view woman is not apart from and independent of man, nor is man aloof from and independent of woman;

¹²For as woman was made from man, even so man is also born of woman; and all [whether male or female go forth] from GOD [as their Author]

¹³Consider for yourselves; is it proper and decent [according to your customs] for a woman to offer prayer to GOD [publicly] with her head uncovered?

¹⁴Does not even native sense of propriety (experience, common sense, reason itself teach you that for a man to wear long hair is a dishonor [humiliating and degrading] to him,

¹⁵But if a woman has long hair, it is her ornament and glory? For her hair is given to her for a covering.

¹⁶Now if anyone is disposed to be argumentative and contentious about this, we hold to and recognized no other custom [in worship] than, nor do the churches of GOD generally.

New Living Translation

1. Pattern yourselves after me [follow my example], as I imitate and follow Christ (the Messiah).

2. I am so glad that you always keep me in your thoughts, and that you are following the teachings I passed on to you.

3. But there is one thing I want you to know: The head of every man is Christ, the head of woman is man, and the head of Christ is GOD.

4. A man dishonors his head if he covers his head while praying or prophesying.

5. But a woman dishonors her head if she prays or prophesies without a covering on her head, for this is the same as shaving her head.

6. Yes, if she refuses to wear a head covering, she should cut off all her hair! But since it is shameful for a woman to have her hair cut or her head shaved, she should wear a covering.

7. A man should not wear anything on his head when worshiping, for man is made in God's image and reflects God's glory. And woman reflects man's glory.

8. For the first man didn't come from woman, but the first woman came from man.

9. And man was not made for the woman, but woman was made for man.

10. For this reason, and because the angels are watching, a woman should wear a covering on her head to show she is under authority.

11. But among the Lord's people, women are not independent of men, and men are not independent.

12. For although the first woman came from man, every other man was born from a woman, and everything comes from God.

13. Judge for yourselves. Is it right for a woman to pray to God in public without covering her head?

14. Isn't it obvious that it's disgraceful for a man to have long hair?

15. And isn't long hair a woman's pride and joy? For it has been given to her as a covering.

16. But if anyone wants to argue about this, I simply say that we have no other custom than this, and neither do God's other churches.

[1] Be ye imitators of me, even as I also am of Christ.

[2] Now I praise you that ye remember me in all things, and hold fast the traditions, even as I delivered them to you.

[3] But I would have you know, that the head of every man is Christ; and the head of the woman is the man; and the head of Christ is God.

[4] Every man praying or prophesying, having his head covered, dishonoreth his head.

[5] But every woman praying or prophesying with her head unveiled dishonoreth her head; for it is one and the same thing as if she were shaven.

[6] For if a woman is not veiled, let her also be shorn: but if it is a shame to a woman to be shorn or shaven, let her be veiled.

[7] For a man indeed ought not to have his head veiled, forasmuch as he is the image and glory of God: but the woman is the glory of the man.

[8] For the man is not of the woman; but the woman of the man:

[9] for neither was the man created for the woman; but the woman for the man:

[10] for this cause ought the woman to have a sign of authority on her head, because of the angels.

[11] Nevertheless, neither is the woman without the man, nor the man without the woman, in the Lord.

[12] For as the woman is of the man, so is the man also by the woman; but all things are of God.

[13] Judge ye in yourselves: is it seemly that a woman pray unto God unveiled?

[14] Doth not even nature itself teach you, that, if a man have long hair, it is a dishonor to him?

[15] But if a woman have long hair, it is a glory to her: for her hair is given her for a covering.

[16] But if any man seemeth to be contentious, we have no such custom, neither the churches of God.

¹Follow my example, just as I follow the example of Christ.

Proper Worship

²I praise you for being faithful in remembering me. I also praise you for staying true to all my teachings, just as I gave them to you.

³ Now I want you to know that the head of every man is Christ. The head of the woman is the man. And the head of Christ is God. ⁴ Every man who prays or prophesies with his head covered brings shame on his head. ⁵ And every woman who prays or prophesies with her head uncovered brings shame on her head. It is just as if her head were shaved.

⁶ What if a woman does not cover her head? She should have her hair cut off. But it is shameful for her to cut her hair or shave it off. So she should cover her head.

⁷ A man should not cover his head. He is the likeness and glory of God. But the woman is the glory of the man.

⁸ The man did not come from the woman. The woman came from the man.

⁹ Also, the man was not created for the woman. The woman was created for the man. ¹⁰ That's why a woman should have her head covered. It shows that she is under authority. She should also cover her head because of the angels.

¹¹ But here is how things are for those who belong to the Lord. The woman is not independent of the man. And the man is not

independent of the woman. [12] The woman came from the man, and the man is born from the woman. But everything comes from God.

[13] You be the judge. Is it proper for a woman to pray to God without covering her head? [14] Suppose a man has long hair. Doesn't the very nature of things teach you that it is shameful? [15] And suppose a woman has long hair. Doesn't the very nature of things teach you that it is her glory? Long hair is given to her as a covering.

[16] If anyone wants to argue about that, we don't have any other practice. And God's churches don't either.

www.ingramcontent.com/pod-product-compliance
Lightning Source LLC
Chambersburg PA
CBHW030530290526
45786CB00004B/1672